More Praise for
We Shoot Typewriters

"*We Shoot Typewriters* is a collection from a seasoned bard that explores the necessary role of poets in our world, the shadow side of ourselves, the search for love, the joy and torment of parenthood, and the absurdity of it all. Each poem takes the reader out into the greater universe, then returns them—whiplashed—with a piece of raw, yet palatable truth."

– **SARAH KOBRINSKY**, Emeryville Poet Laureate

"*We Shoot Typewriters* is a thriller in the De Palma tradition in which there's no particular point except that the hero is flawed, weak, and in terrible danger—and we identify with him completely."

– **ALEXANDRA NAUGHTON**, founder and publisher of Be About It Press

"These are the poems that wake up with wine hangovers after long nights listening to old albums on vinyl—the way music should be heard—while burning through your last pack of cigarettes. These poems are one part heatwave and one part ice-cold beer, with just enough salt and lime to bring down the smack."

– **ALLIE MARINI**, author of *Cliffdiving* and *And When She Tasted Knowledge*

We Shoot Typewriters

Paul Corman-Roberts

NOMADIC PRESS

OAKLAND
111 FAIRMOUNT AVENUE
OAKLAND, CA 94611

BROOKLYN
475 KENT AVENUE #302
BROOKLYN, NY 11249

WWW.NOMADICPRESS.ORG

MASTHEAD
FOUNDING AND MANAGING EDITOR
J. K. FOWLER

ASSOCIATE EDITOR
MICHAELA MULLIN

DESIGN
J. K. FOWLER

MISSION STATEMENT
Nomadic Press is a 501 (C)(3) not-for-profit organization that supports the works of emerging and established writers and artists. Through publications (including translations) and performances, Nomadic Press aims to build community among artists and across disciplines.

SUBMISSIONS
Nomadic Press wholeheartedly accepts unsolicited book manuscripts. To submit your work, please visit www.nomadicpress.org/submissions

DISTRIBUTION
Orders by trade bookstores and wholesalers:
Small Press Distribution,
1341 Seventh Street
Berkeley, CA 94701
spd@spdbooks.org
(510) 524-1668 / (800) 869-7553

We Shoot Typewriters
© 2015 Paul Corman-Roberts

All rights reserved. No part of this book may be reproduced or transmitted in any form or by any means, electronic or mechanical, without written permission from the publisher. Requests for permission to make copies of any part of the work should be sent to: info@nomadicpress.org.

This book was made possible by a loving community of chosen family and friends, old and new.

For author questions or to book a reading at your bookstore, university/school, or alternative establishment, please send an email to info@nomadicpress.org.

Cover artwork by Arthur Johnstone and Livien Yin

Author portrait by Arthur Johnstone

Published by Nomadic Press, 111 Fairmount Avenue, Oakland, CA 94611

Fourth printing, 2019

Printed in the United States of America

LIBRARY OF CONGRESS CATALOGING-IN-PUBLICATION DATA

Corman-Roberts, Paul, 1967 –
Title: *We Shoot Typewriters*
P. CM.
Summary: In *We Shoot Typewriters*, Paul Corman-Roberts brings his dizzying wordplay and emotional anxiety to a fever pitch as he digs into the guts of his community hoping to find the emotional maturity, the vision and the guts to save it.

[1. POETRY/GRIEF. 2. POETRY/FAMILY. 3. AMERICAN GENERAL.] I. III. TITLE.

2015950559
ISBN: 978-0-9966172-1-5

We Shoot Typewriters

Paul Corman-Roberts

NOMADIC PRESS

for el el

CONTENTS

15	THE ACCIDENTAL IMPERIALIST
18	WHAT YOU REALLY WANT TO KNOW
19	SOMEBODIES' RINGIN' THE BELL
21	SCENES FROM A COSMIC WADING POOL
23	COMPLEXIFY MY LOVE
25	SONG OF OUR DIVORCE
27	THE DIALOGUE I REALLY WANT TO HAVE
29	THE RAGGED THERE
30	CANDLES
31	DESPERATELY SEEKING TED
32	WHAT NOBODY REALLY WANTS TO SAY
33	LIKE BYTES OF POSEY THROUGH THE GRINDER; THESE ARE THE DAYS OF OUR CONTRADICTORY EXISTENCES
35	LINES OF SOLITUDE
36	NEW POETRYTHANG BLUES
43	THE BEAST IN ME
45	EL EL
48	MUSTINGS

50   A SOFT PURPLE HELL

51   WHAT I REALLY WANT TO SAY

52   NEW DOG, OLD TRICKS

54   WE SHOOT TYPEWRITERS

THE ACCIDENTAL IMPERIALIST

I'm on to you Shadow man
creeping through the
archetypal funhouse portals
of the subconscious
yes one time too many
a little too fast yeah
and I know who you work
for yeah your boss she
ain't just a son-of-a-bitch
but a real bitch of a bitch
and takes her absurdity queer
up no chaser on no less than
one dozen dialectical levels
simultaneously so you best
watch out next time Creeper man
Moth man I'm going to run straight
for you with my arms wider
than the mansion you found me in
than the desert wash I found you in;
arms wide open to embrace you will
be faced with the prospect of
being stuck for eternity with
a needy clingy poet who will
never let you go and how does that
make you feel shape-shifter
where will you go and what will you do
pull up a chair I hope and sit down
next to me with a spot of some
perhaps powerful tea and maybe
we can work this all out if you
could just please please please
tell me all the stories about all
the things you have seen on
the other side of my galaxy
so that over time my words
then become your words

allowing me to fashion them
into any vehicle I fancy in turn
allowing this see-through barrel
I hold over my head appear
much easier to ride into
the wormhole galleria
perpendicular to a snaking
puffy cloud of sativa
writhing its way down
and across Franklin St
all the way to Brooklyn
but no we skipped
something the past few
years don't match up as
well as I think they ought and
we're missing something, some
bright misguided hope that seemed
without end when our
gritty ass Brigadoon was still
off the map and under radar
expedition ravings where love
seemed possible up on that dim
lit stage but it got all vercocht
somewhere down the way
like everyone was always
in love with the wrong person
just having a hard enough time
getting to the hookup until
we finally got a convention of
these beasts together and Kwan
and MZJ met and fell and are still
falling and still going strong and
the truth is if the rest of this world
falls to shit but these two lovers
are still together it will all have
been worth every damn bit because
that is the kind of love that gives
me more hope than I have
a right to believe in and if you'd

only take a moment to look
through these dazzled beastly
eyes through the eyes of a
conquered shadow man
then you
would
also
love.

WHAT YOU REALLY WANT TO KNOW

"That's so great that you're a poet, but what else do you do?"

Everyone knows
"no one does just poetry."

if they do, politely cough,
turn away
take a few steps
before breaking into
full-fledged escape.

Why all the restlessness? Why all the not owning? Most of us don't want to live where we went to high school. Why do you suppose that is?

We can't avoid your choices.

I know it sounds obvious, but how often do you really acknowledge that fact?

I had the most wonderful line I was going to put on display right here in this piece; I met it at the salon last night, it was sharp and concise, dripping with revelation and wisdom; about 7–9 words long and I think it may have liked me too, but once again, certain that I would certainly remember its imprint, I failed to take down the line's contact info and here I am again, alone, surveying a vast field of freshly fallen snow where everything I dreamed last night is buried.

Yes, we do have to question everything.

To do otherwise would be inhuman.

Being human takes work.

Many people are lazy.

SOMEBODIES' RINGIN' THE BELL

It's Los Angeles
at the door
let's prepare
and let them in
but first- cover
the furniture
and the floors
with plastic

one:
for the ambiance

two:
for the arid dust
sure to blow in
on the winds of
dodgy-ass metaphysics
the warm tingle
and soft caress
of the Santa Ana's
who destroy your life
but only 'cause it
really needs destroying;

and all of it arriving
much faster than
originally anticipated
rolling through
the Doors of our perception now

Dear Lost Angels
welcome to the
great browning
North

Marin;

say goodbye to sequoias
and hello to palm trees.

San Francisco,
say goodbye to fog
and hello to smog.

Oakland,
meet Holly-fucking-wood.

The glare
of winter sunset
will lose its unique
orange particulate glow.

The cosmetic surgery field
will intermingle
its reproductive juices
with the Y combinatory
uterus of Silicon Valley
abetted by the midwifery
of identity politics

and the heat
the heat
the heat
the heat
the heat
the heat
the heat
the heat
the heat
o' the heat
will make us all crazy.

SCENES FROM A COSMIC WADING POOL

and quickly
the cracked
crystalline doors

allowed
the rest of the oxygen
to escape
leaving an atmosphere
composed of
stylized quicksand

up to
the tops of
the backs of
our calves
now weakened
beneath a helium globe.

I send an S. O. S.
to lure you
once you're all in
here with all us we
all know it all

hitching toward
the sun is the place
we disembody and
explains why you have
run short of breath in
your hurry to hear
the sound of
your own
transmogrification.

You will have
to make

your own warm.
I'm sorry.
They don't hand it out
down by the State Building.

They don't hand it out
at the box stores crouching
on the edge of
the colony

and they
won't put it
on layaway either.

You will be cold.
You are cold.
I love you.

COMPLEXIFY MY LOVE

Hard-charging medium
(not like you think)
channeling hard
from beneath the shadow
of Appalachia these
beautiful raw nerves

sweet tragic Jedediah:
opened up now
to transmissions from the rest
of the invisible currency world
(it burns, it burns!)

Jedediah says:
Verbalize for me please
your most recent desires
your most intimate fears
and I know
I ask too much
but I wouldn't have asked
if you hadn't shuffled the cards
with that look in your eye.

You must know
that when you ask for the cross
you must prepare for nails
because the difference
between the truth
and what you perceive
to be the truth
is measured
in your regret
in the valleys
carved along the side
of your oh-so-beautiful face.

I was trying to show you
how tree branches are meant

for holding lights in the night
but I couldn't take my eyes
off the baby possum
frozen so long
I wasn't sure
if it was even real
almost corporeal
until it began
to waddleswim
over and through
the overgrown grass.

There is what is real
and then there is
corresponding illusion.

There is nothing more human
than being unable to tell the difference.

Collectively we prove again
that we are unable to embrace
that we are all
individually
wracked
by the impossible
contradiction of existence
an entire species of demigods
floating in limbo.

The day we open
diplomatic relations
with the mycelium—
the day we choose
to adopt the honey bees
as refugees of war
to own up to the fact
we shouldn't even be here
is the day
we begin
to evolve.

SONG OF OUR DIVORCE

O' spectacle
Where art thou O' spectacle?

Doing the Vicodin Blues Band shuffle no doubt, all over the collective action blueprints with the mid-level managers snickering at the control desk, the very heart of the sun we worship broken down and analyzed from every angle requested on every monitor available.

So now only television snow brims over the cauldron rim and all I want are to slip into my flannel jammies and ensconce myself in a blackened room where I can contemplate a black light replica of the Titanic as she appears now, becoming one with her rust print on the watery floor of an alien planet

accompanied by the disembodied yowling of gutter strewn language poets which magically transform into the sweet, chill aftertaste oasis spring water when filtered through the barren waste of your ashtray manifestos. What I'm trying to say is that a tired old margarita sounds a helluva lot better than your tired new revolution.

It's not our fault if the only option left for you is to cannonball your canon out over the Grand Canyon to the oooh's and aaah's of coyotes, burrows and shape shifters. Congratulations, you are the proud parent to a scrap heap of half-finished lyrics and late '80s Casio sound samples.

The problem with the song you sing is that it receives applause for its applause of others' applause and for that applause, it will certainly garner yet more applause but in the din of all that, your song will not be heard much less negotiate resonance.

True glamour has crawled off to die in a wall space frequented only by the Geraldo Riveras of the social networks, the damage in their wake sublime and unlike any other unique problem, the problem with a line in the sand being that sand moves and shifts in different directions than our eyes move and shift.

My friend, I'm sorry we can't hold each other up anymore, our mutual darkness subsuming our identities to a tune no one wants to hear. Your resentment has become a small price to pay in light of mine having become priceless.

We're at that point in our evolution where we learn all we need to navigate the day's itinerary in seven point five minutes of prefabricated infotainment, a mere four hundred and seventy two point five minutes needed to reach our next fix of fresh infotainment produced, presented and packaged for our easy dot com

                                          part
                                          mental
                                          sization.

So let's make sure and keep a close eye on all the other info-junkies to see if they know as much as we know, let's keep our ears peeled to hear if we can beat them down with our connectedness; to get them to get us off and yes I'm quite aware this a sad victory song we sing

because you can't un-see me Googling every great idea I have to make sure it's really my idea, any more than I can remain tethered to some recognizable sanity within view of your mixed medium collages. There must shelter in a hollowed-out log we can crawl into somewhere around here so long as it has wireless percussion.

I'm sorry the bottom end came undone, but the top became so, so long ago and what I'm asking for here is for you to give me just one more chance to score us a date with the Courtney Love of the small press I swear if can do that then I can make all, all, all of our nightmares come true, because I know you're tired of asking nicely, and quite frankly, I am, too.

THE DIALOGUE I REALLY WANT TO HAVE

Back when I was young
and strung out
as opposed to old
and wrapped tight
I could talk to birds.

I'd wander out
into my backyard
at some godless
but all-too-human hour
and could hear
the rhythms
the patterns
the melodies
the call and response
the jazz
in the songs
of the desert finches
who ruled Las Vegas
in its semi-darkened AM ecstasies.

I was seduced by
the cadence
the complexity
to the point of seeking out
my own wet
acid-drenched
whistle
my own raptor voice
and so would attempt
to replicate the exact song
of the finch who sat
just feet above my head
in the nearest jumble
of dry branches.

What I realized as I did this
was that she always
patiently waited
for me to finish
my attempted trills
before she would then
spin out a chirping
tweeting retort
that ran circles
around my
dusted imagination
that left my tongue
        dizzy
my brain
        nauseous
my eyes
        twirling

but
we were in dialogue
human and bird
raptor spawn alike.

I could do shit like that
in those days.

I suppose I'm wiser now.

I often wonder
how much
that is worth.

THE RAGGED THERE

All that ripples
in the latest world
are sand dunes, parched
        cracked
        ripples
of lack.

He celebrates
w/abandon
w/anticipation
of inundation

she is already
more hyper aware
of the importance
of water relative
to my awareness
when I was her age.

She watches me go outside
and stand in it for awhile;
watches me lift my face to it
for awhile.

I look at her
and motion for her to join me
and she does so
if somewhat flinchingly;
the smile of her mouth
perfect in its honesty.
I've had my share of this.

My fear
is that in a day not far away
she will need to record these moments
as much for herself
and not merely her children.

CANDLES

Do you know why candles are perfect?
Because when you squint at them
Just the right way
They look like the number one.
This one is made up of three components:
Wax, wick, and flame.
Without these components
A candle cannot function
Therefore, a candle cannot be.
The wax molecules in the candle
Look around to see only
their fellow wax molecules.
And declare their sum total to be wax.
"We look like wax
We act like wax
Thus we are wax."
But in fact they are a candle.
Someday they will realize this.
They will hear the panicked rumors of an impending flame.
When the flame gets close
The wax molecules will do things they had not dreamed of.
Their foundations will become less solid they thought they were;
Their patchwork reality more fluid;
Their interactions and engagements occur at speeds
Faster than thought possible.
And as always, they will seek their own level
And become one with the flame
Etheric
A candle cycle complete.
And if you think this poem is about candles
Then you're still just part of the wax.

DESPERATELY SEEKING TED

There can be no sleep
for us on an evening
so fraught with chill
and agenda.

You only get this
one chance to see
the wormhole where
the darkness prevailed.

There is too much juice
running through the circuits
of the mist-strewn enclave
sleep every bit as effervescent

every bit as elusive
every bit as precious
as love
when all barter
turns half hearted
in the face of
intractable faces.

and still the question comes
though sure we had it ditched:

"What's goin' on here in this room?"

I don't know man.
What IS going on in here?
I guess you are man,
I guess
you are.

WHAT NOBODY REALLY WANTS TO SAY

No one explains anything anymore.

You're just supposed to know.

Didn't you know?

What's wrong with you?

Don't tell anyone.

Don't tell anyone that nobody knows anything and it will all be okay, okay?

LIKE BYTES OF POSEY THROUGH THE GRINDER; THESE ARE THE DAYS OF OUR CONTRADICTORY EXISTENCES

You are clearly
        almost Spanish
        and pretty sure
        he wants my sandwich
This stuff happens all around me
        where she was just
        standing in the bathroom stall
        talking on her cell
You too can be
        not just a writer
        but an organizer
        but not just a writer
        or organizer
        but a leader
        a leader of men
Wait . . . only men?
        OF MEN!
        right, yes
A contributor to some new neo-ism
        isn't that kinda sexist?
        at the risk of coming off
        insincere
I'm ambidextrous in response
        to your exquisite Suarez
        which seriously kicked my ass
        just like one, two, five
Was a game changer
        when she chirped
        "three, sir"
And I can live in a world
        where I'm a second husband
        with a part-time wife

**But you still need a scorecard
        in a world
        where no one scores**

LINES OF SOLITUDE

My galaxy for a planet of Orpheus I.

My planet for a city of singing poets.

My city for a single lover in my orbit.

Light does not apologize for its awkward presence in dark matters.
        And why should it?
                Everyone knows it's nobody's fault,
                      the invisible weight of these
                arrangements.

The infinite death bout
between appetite
and vanity?

We lust.
        We transact.
                We are disgusted.
And we didn't even have sex.
What could be more German?

Oh what spectacles can we build
for public consumption now?

Just some strange
physical hustle
of intermingled
mashed up identity
that didn't quite take.

Sure we are sad, but secretly:
                            more comfortable alone.

"We mean what we say, but we don't say what we mean."

– Spencer Reece

NEW POETRYTHANG BLUES

I don't care
what the neighbors
say this languid,
lolling conversion
from NIMBY
to YIMBY
YES IN MY BACK YARD
Is the heart and soul of New Orleans
chewing up line 1
explainin' about how
Jackson Square gumbo
gets spicier
the further west its delivered.
reckons the iconoclast
riding shotgun
in ironic class
Better dying
thru chemistry

People talkin' all around this poetrythang is gonna be big I tells ya, you're all gonna blow up into these big, big genius stars any day now target will make huge offers for only the best of the best to staff their pop up poetry installations in the aisles where there used to be CDs and DVDs right next to a life size cardboard cutout of Beyonce and J getting it on oohh, never you mind all that poetrythang 'cuz the Fukushima Super Wal-Mart just washed up on Stinson Beach and oh man you wouldn't believe the savings now half off on all self generating holograms for skinny jeans and handlebar mustaches and oh thank you thank you lord god Tsunami you wouldn't believe what mama's been trying to do to us she's on the run like the man said, she's on the lam, she's on wanted posters in every dark alley, under every bed and damned if you wasn't the one who let her in here anyway, wanting to cleanse yourself in her psychic shower of pheromone pollen all of it slip siding across the great primal pond and when it shows for load-in we must immediately guide it to the ministry of surrender where the rock stars and porn stars go to give up, their better years behind them, their legacies grown larger but more ephemeral with a sidelined mythology

But they don't stop.

I don't feel;
like I can trust poetry at all.
I always feel poetry
has got one foot out the door.
I feel like poetry and I
have commitment issues.

but we don't stop
until we do

stop?

Haven't you figured out that our children's school textbooks are thoroughly vetted by the National Security Agency?

Has anyone explained to you that you're an angel who is really, really high on carcinogens?

Have you happened to notice the virus sitting above us in the food chain?

Doesn't it seem like the other side of town is haunted? Or at least very poorly lit?

And were you able to keep track of every person you sexually objectified on your way here?

And when exactly was the last time you forgot to masturbate?

And how is it that so many mad ranting street prophets somehow magically evolve into the sage elders of what is left of civilization?

And why is it that so many of our younger brilliant,

underground poets invest so much of
their valuable time crucifying all the older, somewhat less
brilliant above board poets?

Because.

There can't merely be cleverness
There can't merely
Be virtuosity for virtuosity's sake
There must be humor
And humor means
Someone's going to get hurt

There must be humor
Or we will drag
The corpse of Academia
Around with us forever

And maybe that's why
We continue
This game as business of usual

What is the passing of all these
obscenely gorgeous moments
But the continuous interlude
Between all our lyrical preludes
Where any of us
Just hope to break out
Our oh-so-tasteful galleries
of Agit-porn

Don't get me wrong
I appreciate the Romance of
Remembering our individual
And collective high points
On a timeline
Pointing to a source
We all came here
To search for

An Easter-egg hunt
For common consciousness

By poets who were the first lawyers
Poet who were the first tag artists
Poets who were the first clergy
In an Eden
Of their making
But if it is true prayer
You seek than you must
Take the *hajj* of your life
Into that big theater
For hymnals and chants
Of the interior body

Some poets
Just don't have
What it takes
To love Lilith
Though she's there
For us all
Don't complain that she's
A hard bitch she's
The medicine you need
I know 'cause I saw
A father riding on the train
with his baby girl
And he wanted so badly to be loved
By all the young teen dreamers
Dolled up for the season

But the baby girl is squirming
in his arms
She's breaking his cool
Down in front
Of the hotties
A man un-babed by his baby
And it ain't the first time
And it won't be the last that

This temple of public transit
Careens down the path of
The secular left hand
One more time baby

Nah, some poets
Just don't know their Lil
You don't have to ball her
To love her
Break it down
Like you mean it brother
After all
Isn't sex just another form of prayer?
Reminding us how close we lounge
To the reptiles inside the big theater
And when that is all said and done
There is still the passing moment
Still
For this moment
Hovering right here
In front of your eyes
Still crying out
For your attention
Still crying out
for your naming
And once you engage
in this practice of naming
You'll never be asked to stop
You'll be lost
In a wide open mouth
Lost in a process of
Smoking
Singing
Sucking
Licking
Eating
Gnashing
Swallowing
Breathing

Pissing
Shitting
Flowing
Becoming
All in search
Of a construct
That may or may not belong to God
And regardless of that possibility
You must somehow always remember
That it is always a two way street

And knowing that
Would you still like
to record the death of the West?
Then please go right ahead and
Take a number and get in the line
Because it is work and work alone
Which will set the self-analyzing
Monkey free in this elegy
Poet, seduce thyself
And know the inner Heaven cylinder
Is the place you will see
Through constructs

I tried to be an atheist
I tried not to believe
But ever since dawn light came
To the Mojave red lands
This is one exorcism
That never ends
And language poetry thy
Cup runneth over
And spills out
Into the great
Los Angeles basin
With no regard
To whom you may drown
Along the way
Yet the survivors

Will be stronger
In the end for this flood
Over the world's stage
But the great curtain
Remains the great colonizer
of context beneath which
The wizard alas,
truly is naked and horny
And leering at Dorothy

But at least we can be thankful
For the United Auto Workers
Who remind us
Each and every day
Why Fast Freddy Hegel
And Crazy Karlo Marx
keep hanging around
Like the true jazz men they are
Riffing the apocalypse fantastic
From the edge
Of their felt porkpie specials
Each and Every day
All the while asking
That we crucify them
Each and every day
So that some older
Somewhat less brilliant
Poet's prophecies
Might
come
true

.

THE BEAST IN ME

She's my baby and I love her always
no never could have drowned her
but she's a freak you know, a mutant
she don't grow slow like the rest of them
no she ages one year for every month

And now she's fifteen-going-on-thirty
and we're hanging out in the back yard
spending quality time together
and some things are unnatural

Like the scent of plum and cherry blossoms
filling the air in this same backyard
for five consecutive days in February

And being fifteen-going-on-thirty
and having to let her grow up
and having to let her be a grown up
and make grown up mistakes

I worry that she is drinking or taking drugs
with wild people
and maybe she's been having unsafe sex
with wild people
and maybe these are the same wild people
I trusted to take care of her in the first place

And I know I'm just this sad
old fuddy with the impending
empty-nest-syndrome blues
and that even after all the growing pains
and all the years she will pretend I don't exist
or acknowledge that her father
knows anything at all

There will eventually come
epic reunions and celebrations.
      between us

there will be those quiet moments of gratitude.
        between us
there will be love.
and remembering.

But my beastie,
won't be my baby anymore.
From the moment we were closest
we were always fading
from each other.
and the older we both get
the less and less we will know each other.

Until eventually
there will come that inevitable day
when we look each other in the eyes
and we won't know each other at all.

EL EL

> *"One only loves that which one does
> not entirely possess."* – Proust

I never sleep those nights before the day you fly so very far away from me and so it is on this frozen, lightless morning with your lovely oval face melting into the pillows. The forever furrow in your brow becoming ether; your porcelain truth radiating in this darkest of darks where the last memory of anything worth living for clings by the merest hangnail to the wall tissues of the cosmic uterus with more desperation than any creation borne until this moment.

Begin decorating what you need the rest of your time here to look like. Not want. Need. Take the time to know the difference.

I would still love you even if you willfully transformed your honey streaked aura into a dust bunny living among the rocks in the corner of my eye. I would still fantasize about your wispy non-substantiation. I would still touch myself in inappropriate places and wonder what that would look like and I realize because it is real

                      and it is true
                      and it is love

that I would not care
what that would look like.

            CUT CHOP SLICE SEVER
            CUT CHOP SLICE SEVER
            CUT CHOP SLICE SEVER

            GATHER GATHER GATHER
            GATHER GATHER GATHER
            GATHER GATHER GATHER

I took you out of this world and I can bring you back into it. Death cannot save you from my love. I need you to believe that more than I need to believe that. How profound is it that we can so violently and completely assault each other's boundaries

without coming into actual physical contact with our target?
How is love even born into such a world?

This is the source of our hope; that we don't know. But it
really happens. Love is born into our world and we never really
know how. If we discovered how, would it really, truly fuck
everything over?

I suspect real love is when we take all the permanent ink we
can gather and draw in each other's wrinkles, scars, liver spots,
warts, back fat and stretch marks before the world does.

Your wormhole dance will always only ever be your wormhole
dance alone, but I still try for convergence, for long term
intercourse on every possible plane: a totally different kind of
milestone high club.

>
> CUT CHOP SLICE SEVER
> CUT CHOP SLICE SEVER
> CUT CHOP SLICE SEVER
>
> GATHER GATHER GATHER
> GATHER GATHER GATHER
> GATHER GATHER GATHER

Why would we ever stop playing with Prometheus matches?
Not knowing WHAT is on the other side, but simply that
there IS another side. So go ahead and fumble with them. Our
fingers will always be furious with this fire, no matter how
many times you burn out, no matter how many times your dust
coats my teeth; the existence of said dust signaling:

our arrival
at an afterword
to an epilogue
where I can sense
the hardening
in your stance
toward my words

where I can feel a resolve
in your protest
in your prone
in your pull
in that smallest singularity
of our Shiva fold
is where you will find me
hustling for a back stage pass
for that one peek
behind the magical curtain
for the memory of the taste
of your pungent aroma
pulled from your dark matter
calling me back to a dance
set to soundless music
which never repeats
but which is always familiar
between the divining
and the archiving
in this crushing gravitational
singularity

        CUT CHOP SLICE SEVER
        CUT CHOP SLICE SEVER
        CUT CHOP SLICE SEVER

        GATHER GATHER GATHER
        GATHER GATHER GATHER
        GATHER GATHER GATHER

in this infinitesimal fold of Shiva
lays the great soupy muddle of something called "us."
I don't want

    Soft

I want
I need
you.

MUSTINGS

people understand
        lo-tech
                under grounders don't
look for the glossy
        parts of that
                cesspool punk
which are better than
        sexist periodicals
                like *Minimum Rock and Roll*

rejected from
    NY Quarterly
            doesn't have "the rep"
    yuppie privilege
is just butt hurt

You can hate people all you want
        like the *New Yorker* or *Harpers* or *The Nation*
                the assumption others
        have it so easy
is not their job
        to make "hard workers" comfortable
                they are not going away
                        any of them

the first signal of collapse:
        one day she will say "get a job"
        fall into that same old despair
baggage makes us feel that way

My journey
        my strife
my angst
        my crisis
my fucking shit
        can't spare the empathy

And he will hate me

        before long
                it's all booze, cigarettes
chameleoning
        for the latest mate
            screeeeech

I don't really care if its ass kissing or not
        good editors close read yo

I told him that shit is wrong
        I've been the cuckold
            I know

My hate has to be earned
        even by racists

A SOFT PURPLE HELL

The light and shadow
of an early Sunday evening
are still the same
after all these years.

On our nights of night
there is always a downpour
an impossible mission
needing to be finished by dawn

before the clang clang
of the markets
before the swelling of
the morning news theme music

before the last wisp of smoke
from the last cigarette
coils off into a turbulent future
among the morning's raindrops.

So it was the night before
my first day of high school.
So it shall be the night before
I make the half-century watermark

and Sunday remains the same
the same cloaked diffusion of time
making its awareness of itself
an ocean that swallows us whole
that levels us anonymous
to all but ourselves

a soft purple hell
the same swelling and tide
of light and shadow
as all those years ago.

WHAT I REALLY WANT TO SAY

Dear prospective lover who lives thousands of miles away,

I can smell your pheromones from here: It all makes sense in just a snapshot of images, words, and shared cultural compatibility; comparing obsessions, testing the depths of each other's geeked out poetic soul and continuing to find resonance and the complete denial that someone living within the boundaries or our existence can't merely be shut off at our earliest convenience and when we put it all together it almost forms the outline of something that looks familiar, forms the outline of an image we don't want to admit we've been searching high and low for, so please don't look too closely at the pieces that don't quite match up.

We'll be able to patchwork those gaps in the years with promises of open communication lines and extra-hard, internal emotional work and honesty and ego death and enough of that will lead to some of that magic no, that eternal lucky break, that well deserved luck, no?

NEW DOG, OLD TRICKS

It rains less and less
here in California.

When it can
finally
be bothered
to precipitate again
it always comes
in the dark of morning
in furious dashes of
whipping sheet water
curtains unfolding
across the sun-baked,
piss-and-shit-concrete city.

Always in the dark of morning
when it's me and the hound
out on patrol.

We knew what we were in for.
It had to be done.
But nothing can prepare you
for this kind of dousing.

The hound in his floral print rain coat;
the indignity of it
emphasizing his sad Beagle eyes;
me in a leather football helmet
and three of the bulkiest cotton layers
laying around that I could pile
onto my barrel chest;
all of it useless
beneath the wide open faucet of Heaven.

You learn to keep moving in the rain.
Even the marking hound knows this:

Don't stop.

Don't ever stop
long enough
to let the chill
hook its tendrils
into the angel tears
running across your forehead
and down your cheek
as if they were
a defective car windshield
with demented windshield wipers:
never let the unnatural caress
of an elemental turn cold
when in the midst
of travailing
the destination is the thing:

even the marking hound knows this to be true.

WE SHOOT TYPEWRITERS
for VK III

Moonlight glinting
off your words
down by Lakeshore
a Midnight open mic
for an audience
of one somewhere
across the far shore
shifting in the dark
refusing to come into focus
you resisting the urge to call out
and this is all so familiar, isn't it?
you've done this before
it's not your first incarnation
and you allow yourself to suppose
that it might be
the dream
the nightmare.

Yes, the divide between you
and your shadow other
is the same as the divide
between you and your waking
other
merely transposed
recast upon
a shifting diaspora
fraught with every kind of dagger:
verbal
enabling
compulsive
daggers in the night
daggers in the day.

The blood smeared and dried
across our wasted husks
tells its own story.
I know the words get tired.

I know the words get tiring.
At the end of our ropes
that is all there ever is:
all these vaporous
wispy, substanceless
ephemeral nothings
their summarized wakes
crying:
"What Ho There Scribe"
trader of the invisible
commodities that we
already have too much of . . .

. . . they shoot typewriters, don't they?
Don't they still?
Clearly they have been proliferating of late
breeding beyond all means of sustainability
and maybe the city council should initiate
a hunting season to bring the population down.
It's just that we're starting to feel
threatened by them don't you see?

This is one of those
Situationist situations
where a proliferation of words
leads to their morphing
from weapons of beauty
into weapons of conformity
daggers turned inward and
against their users some dark
magic of the markets triggering
their reversal; daggers in the water
daggers on land, daggers between
me and my shadow other, daggers
between me and the terrace I
descended from; all of them
inscribed with the word "truth."

And truth

is a moment
for all artists;
the one moment
why we became artists
to have the chutzpah
to call ourselves mirrors
worthy of human reflection
worthy of human truth;
because there was
that one moment
when the Cosmos
winked at each one of us
but only when we were alone
a wink that was meant
only for you
and you
and you
and you
and you
and you
and you
and you
and you
and you
and you
and you
and you

and

you alone

and

we spend the rest of our lives
trying to convince all the other mirrors
and bystanders and whoever will listen
that it really happened to us just that way
and then we put that all together

until we have a cacophony of mirrors
recreating the facsimile of a sentient
blinking, flirting, farting universe
instead of engaging
in real flirting and farting
and even sentient blinking

And despite the evidence of this
happening all around us
all the time, we still have the bystanders
still wondering after all this time
why it always seems like we are always
on drugs, or even worse, in love.

They still shoot typewriters, don't they?

I need a hunting partner
to either swim, wade, or
circumnavigate with
to the far shore
to tip toe through
the dagger tulip fields with

these being the most uncertain
of partnerships but also
the most promising of friendships.

ACKNOWLEDGEMENTS

Thank you to those who have previously published a few of the pieces within this collection: "Somebodies' Ringin' the Bell," *Be About It* (June 2015); "Song of Our Divorce," *Out of Our Magazine* (Fall 2014); and "Candles," *The Dead Mule School of Literature* (Spring 2012).

PAUL CORMAN-ROBERTS is the author of the chapbooks *19th Street Station* (Full of Crow Chaps, 2011), *Notes From An Orgy* (Paper Press 2014), and *We Shoot Typewriters* (Nomadic Press 2015.) He is a co-founder of Oakland's Beast Crawl Literary Festival where he lives with his family, teaches, and dreams up hijinx and shenanigans designed to undermine the dominant paradigm. His first full-length poetry collection, *Bone Moon Palace* is forthcoming from Nomadic Press.